GALAXIES

SPACE-THEMED RECIPES

by Jane Yates

Minneapolis, Minnesota

Credits

Cover and title page, © Triff/Shutterstock and © New Africa/Shutterstock and © Sanit Fuangnakhon/ Shutterstock; Background images, angel_nt/Adobe Stock; backgroundgraph, Lifestyle Graphic/Adobe Stock; 5 top left, DestinaDesign/Shutterstock.com; 5 right middle, Christos Georghiou/Shutterstock.com; 6, © NASA; 8 bottom, ESA/Hubble & NASA/Creative Commons; 10, © pioneer111/Adobe Stock; 12 bottom, elements of this image furnished by NASA. Triff /Shutterstock.com; 14 bottom, NASA, ESA, and The Hubble Heritage Team (STScI/AURA)/Public Domain; 16, © Michelle/Adobe Stock; 18 bottom left, NASA, ESA, and the Hubble Heritage Team (STScI/AURA)-ESA/Hubble Collaboration. Acknowledgement: B. Whitmore (Space Telescope Science Institute) and James Long (ESA/Hubble)/Creative Commons; 19, © grey/Adobe Stock; 20 bottom left, HST/ NASA/ESA/Public Domain; 20 bottom middle, KKolaczynski/Creative Commons; 22 top right, NASA/Public Domain; all other photos ©Austen Photography

Bearport Publishing Company Product Development Team

Publisher: Jen Jenson; Director of Product Development: Spencer Brinker; Editorial Director: Allison Juda; Editor: Cole Nelson; Editor: Tiana Tran; Production Editor: Naomi Reich; Art Director: Kim Jones; Designer: Kayla Eggert; Designer: Steve Scheluchin; Production Specialist: Owen Hamlin

Statement on Usage of Generative Artificial Intelligence

Bearport Publishing remains committed to publishing high-quality nonfiction books. Therefore, we restrict the use of generative AI to ensure accuracy of all text and visual components pertaining to a book's subject. See BearportPublishing.com for details.

Produced for Bearport Publishing by BlueAppleWorks Inc.

Managing Editor for BlueAppleWorks: Melissa McClellan
Art Director: T.J. Choleva
Photo Research: Jane Reid

Library of Congress Cataloging-in-Publication Data

Names: Yates, Jane author
Title: Galaxies : space-themed recipes / by Jane Yates.
Description: Minneapolis, Minnesota : Bearport Publishing, [2026] | Series:
    Space-licious! Out-of-this-world recipes | "Create!" | Includes
    bibliographical references and index.
Identifiers: LCCN 2025004590 (print) | LCCN 2025004591 (ebook) | ISBN
    9798895770320 library binding | ISBN 9798895771495 ebook
Subjects: LCSH: Cooking--Juvenile literature |
    Galaxies--Miscellanea--Juvenile literature | LCGFT: Cookbooks
Classification: LCC TX652.5 .Y375 2026 (print) | LCC TX652.5 (ebook) |
    DDC 641.5--dc23/eng/20250227
LC record available at https://lccn.loc.gov/2025004590
LC ebook record available at https://lccn.loc.gov/2025004591

Copyright © 2026 Bearport Publishing Company. All rights reserved. No part of this publication may be reproduced in whole or in part, stored in any retrieval system, or transmitted in any form or by any means, electronic, mechanical, photocopying, recording, or otherwise, without written permission from the publisher. Bearport Publishing is a division of FlutterBee Education Group.

For more information, write to Bearport Publishing, 3500 American Blvd W, Suite 150, Bloomington, MN 55431.

CONTENTS

Space-licious! 4

Celestial Nachos 6

Popcorn Cluster Galaxies 8

Cosmic Cheese Spiral 12

Galaxy Bark 14

Galactic Punch 18

Cosmic Ice Cream 20

Meet a Hungry Astronaut 22
Glossary 23
Index 24
Read More 24
Learn More Online 24
About the Author 24

SPACE-LICIOUS!

Let's learn about space and cooking at the same time! How would you like to try a cheesy cosmic spiral or colorful popcorn cluster galaxies? With this book, you can make six delicious, out-of-this-world recipes. Let's blast off!

Measuring liquid ingredients

- Use a measuring cup with a spout. This makes it easier to pour liquids without spilling.
- Always set the measuring cup on a flat surface.
- When adding liquid, bend down so your eye is level with the measurements on the cup. This ensures you have the right amount.

Measuring dry ingredients

- Scoop the ingredients with the correct size measuring cup or measuring spoon.
- Level off the top with the back of a butter knife or another straight edge. This will ensure you have an accurate amount.

Ingredients

Most of these recipes can be made with things you probably already have in your kitchen. Before you start each recipe, make sure you have all the ingredients you need. It's a good idea to set your ingredients and tools on the counter before you begin.

Microwave safety

Each microwave works a little differently, so ask an adult to help show you how to use yours. Be sure to use only dishes that are safe for the microwave, such as glass or ceramic. Never use metal or aluminum foil in the microwave. After cooking, carefully check that a dish isn't too hot before taking it out.

Allergy Alert!

Recipes that include wheat or dairy are marked with a special symbol. Please use a safe substitute ingredient if you need to.

 Wheat

 Dairy

 Always ask for an adult's help with knives and when using the oven or stove.

CELESTIAL NACHOS

Galaxies are made up of stars, planets, and huge clouds of gas and dust, all held together by **gravity**. In these **celestial** nachos, you'll use cheese to hold together the different ingredients. You can imagine them as stars, planets, and clouds of gas clustered together in the night sky.

Ingredients

- Tortilla chips
- ½ cup shredded cheddar cheese
- ¼ cup cherry tomatoes
- 1 Tbsp sliced olives

Allergy Alert!

Equipment

- A microwave-safe plate
- A knife for your adult helper
- Oven mitts

The galaxy M83 is 15 million light-years from Earth.

1. Place enough tortilla chips on a plate to cover it in an even layer.

2. Sprinkle shredded cheese evenly over the tortilla chips.

3. Ask an adult to use a knife to cut the cherry tomatoes in half. Then, place the cut tomatoes and olives on top of the cheese.

4. Microwave the plate for 30 seconds.

5. Using oven mitts, remove the plate from the microwave.

6. Let your nachos cool slightly, and then enjoy your celestial snack!

NOTE: Be careful when you take the plate out of the microwave. It may be hot!

POPCORN CLUSTER GALAXIES

Sometimes, galaxies form in groups called clusters. These clusters also contain a mysterious mass called **dark matter**. We can't see this matter, but we know it exists because of the way it interacts with gravity. Make your own popcorn clusters to form a galactic snack, with chocolate drizzled on top to symbolize the dark matter.

Ingredients

- 4 cups popped popcorn
- 2 cups mini marshmallows
- 2 Tbsp butter or margarine, plus a little extra
- ¼ cup mini candy-covered chocolate candies
- 2 Tbsp sprinkles or other small candies
- ¼ cup chocolate chips

Allergy Alert!

Studying galaxy clusters helps scientists learn more about dark matter and dark energy.

Equipment

★ A baking sheet
★ Parchment paper
★ 1 large mixing bowl
★ 2 microwave-safe bowls
★ A mixing spoon
★ A small spoon

1. Line a baking sheet with parchment paper and set it aside.

2. Then, put the popped popcorn into a large mixing bowl.

3. Add the mini marshmallows and butter or margarine to a microwave-safe bowl.

4. Microwave the marshmallow and butter mixture for 30 seconds. Then, remove the bowl from the microwave and stir with a spoon until the ingredients are fully combined and smooth.

5 Pour the melted marshmallow mixture over the popcorn.

6 Gently stir with a spoon to combine the popcorn and marshmallow mixture until the popcorn is evenly coated.

7 Mix in the candy-coated chocolates. Stir in the other candy and sprinkles to ensure all ingredients are well mixed.

8 Lightly coat your hands with margarine or butter. Then, grab a handful of the popcorn mixture from the bowl and pack it into a fist-sized ball. Place the clusters on the prepared baking sheet. Repeat until all the popcorn is used.

9 Add the chocolate chips to another microwave-safe bowl and heat for 30 seconds. Stir the chocolate with a small spoon. Repeat heating for 10 seconds, stirring in between, until the chocolate is almost completely melted. Then, carefully remove the bowl from the microwave and stir again until the chocolate is smooth.

10 Use the spoon to drizzle the melted chocolate over the popcorn clusters. Before serving, allow them to sit until the chocolate has hardened. Enjoy your delicious popcorn cluster galaxies!

COSMIC CHEESE SPIRAL

Galaxies come in different shapes. One of the most common kinds is the spiral galaxy. These galaxies have a tightly packed center with spiral arms that curve outward like a **pinwheel**. Create your own cheesy bread spiral with arms that **radiate** from the center like a tasty galaxy!

Ingredients

- Prepared pizza dough
- A small amount of all-purpose flour
- 1 cup shredded mozzarella cheese
- 1 Tbsp dried oregano
- ½ cup pesto, marinara, or other sauce of your choice

Allergy Alert!

Equipment

- A bowl
- A pizza pan or baking sheet
- Parchment paper
- A butter knife
- A spoon

Our galaxy, the Milky Way, is one of billions of spiral galaxies in the universe.

12

1. Place the pizza dough in a bowl and let it **proof** for an hour.

2. Have an adult **preheat** the oven to 425°F (215°C). Line a pizza pan with parchment paper.

3. Lightly **dust** a clean work surface with flour to prevent sticking.

4. Next, turn out the dough from the bowl, and ask an adult to help you cut it into four equal pieces using a butter knife.

5. Roll, stretch, and twist each piece of dough into a strand about 7 in. (18 cm) long. Lay the strands on the pizza pan so they are connected at the center and curve outward in a spiral galaxy shape.

6. Sprinkle shredded mozzarella cheese over the dough. Bake in the oven for 15 minutes or until the edges are golden brown.

7. Ask an adult to carefully remove the pan from the oven. Then, sprinkle oregano over the spiral.

8. Spoon pesto, marinara, or another favorite sauce on top of the spiral. Munch on your snack by breaking off one arm at a time.

GALAXY BARK

Galaxies that don't have a clearly defined shape are known as **irregular** galaxies. They may be round or long, but most often they just look like blobs. Make your own tasty irregular galaxy by swirling colorful melted chocolate with candy stars and planets. *Yum!*

Ingredients

- 1 cup semi-sweet or dark chocolate chips
- 1 cup white chocolate chips
- Red and blue food coloring
- Assorted small candies and sprinkles

Allergy Alert!

Equipment

- A baking sheet
- Parchment paper
- A medium microwave-safe bowl
- 4 spoons
- 2 small microwave-safe bowls

Irregular galaxies often have dark patches filled with gas and dust that may some day form new stars.

14

1. Line the baking sheet with parchment paper.

2. Place the semi-sweet or dark chocolate chips into the medium-sized microwave-safe bowl.

3. Heat the chocolate in the microwave for 30 seconds. Remove and stir with a spoon. Repeat the process, heating in 10-second **intervals** and stirring each time, until the chocolate is completely smooth.

4. Next, pour the melted chocolate onto the prepared baking sheet and use a spoon to spread it into a long oval shape.

5 Divide the white chocolate chips evenly between two small microwave-safe bowls.

6 Follow the directions from Step 3 to melt the chocolate in each bowl.

7 Add a few drops of blue food coloring to one bowl of melted white chocolate and stir until the color is evenly mixed in.

8 Repeat Step 7 with red food coloring in the second bowl of melted white chocolate to make pink-colored chocolate.

9. Next, spoon **dollops** of the pink and blue chocolate onto the dark chocolate oval.

10. Use a clean spoon to gently swirl the colors together, creating a galactic effect.

11. Decorate the chocolate galaxy with assorted candies and sprinkles to represent stars and planets.

12. Put the baking sheet in the fridge for about an hour, until the chocolate hardens.

13. Once the chocolate has fully set, break it into small pieces and enjoy your irregular, but delicious, galaxy!

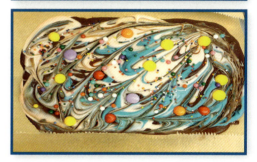

GALACTIC PUNCH

Sometimes, galaxies drift too close to each other and **collide**. When this happens, two galaxies become one, mixing their gases, stars, and planets together. Make some galactic punch where colorful ice cubes melt and blend, just like the swirling gases of merging galaxies.

Ingredients

- Assorted fruit juices of different colors
- 1 lemon, sliced
- 1 lime, sliced
- 1 orange, sliced
- A 2.1 qt. (2-L) bottle of lemon-lime soda

Equipment

- An ice cube tray
- A large punch bowl
- A spoon
- A ladle
- Glasses

It takes millions of years for two galaxies to collide and form into a new galaxy.

1. Fill an ice cube tray with different fruit juices.

2. Carefully place the tray into the freezer for about 3 hours to allow the juice to freeze completely.

3. Once the juice is frozen, turn the ice cube tray upside down over the punch bowl and twist the tray to release the colorful ice cubes into the bowl.

4. Add most of the lemon, lime, and orange slices on top of the ice cubes. Set aside a few slices as **garnish** for later.

5. Pour the bottle of lemon-lime soda over the ice cubes and fruit slices. Stir gently.

6. Use a ladle to pour the punch into glasses. Ask an adult to cut a slit halfway through the saved fruit slices. Slide a slice onto each glass, and enjoy your galactic drink!

COSMIC ICE CREAM

Galaxies get their colors from the swirl of gases and stars within the space objects. Mostly blue stars may tinge a galaxy blue, while red stars will make it red. Some galaxy clusters have a mix of both red and blue stars. Create your own colorful cosmic ice cream with swirls of red and blue!

Ingredients

* A 14-oz (414-mL) can sweetened condensed milk
* 1 tsp vanilla extract
* A 1 pt. (473-mL) container heavy whipping cream
* Red and blue food coloring
* Sprinkles

Allergy Alert!

Equipment

* 3 mixing spoons
* 3 small mixing bowls
* 1 large mixing bowl
* A whisk
* A loaf pan
* A butter knife
* Plastic wrap or foil
* An ice cream scoop
* An ice cream bowl

The hottest stars burn blue and white. The coolest-burning stars appear red.

20

1. Stir the condensed milk and vanilla extract in a small bowl until well combined. Set aside.

2. In the large bowl, mix the whipping cream using a **whisk** in a side-to-side motion. Continue until the cream forms soft peaks and stays on the whisk when lifted.

3. Next, fold the condensed milk mixture into the whipped cream by making big scooping motions with the spoon. Be gentle to avoid knocking air out of the cream. Then, divide the mixture equally between two small mixing bowls.

4. Add red food coloring to one bowl and blue to the other. Stir gently until the colors are evenly mixed.

5. Using two spoons, alternate adding scoops of each colored mixture into a loaf pan. Use a butter knife to gently swirl the colors together for a cosmic effect.

6. Cover the pan with plastic wrap or foil and place it in the freezer for at least 3 hours, or until the ice cream is firm.

7. Once frozen, scoop the ice cream into bowls, top with sprinkles, and enjoy your colorful, cosmic treat!

MEET A HUNGRY ASTRONAUT

Peggy Whitson made history as the first woman to command the International Space Station. She also became NASA's first female Chief Astronaut. During her missions, Peggy enjoyed eating hamburgers, but space burgers look a little different! To avoid crumbs, astronauts use tortillas instead of buns for their burgers.

Peggy Whitson with her creatively prepared space burger.

Make a Tortilla Space Burger

1. Fold a tortilla in quarters. Unfold it.

2. Using the fold lines as guides, place a burger patty in the bottom right quarter of the tortilla.

3. Place condiments on the bottom left quarter. Add lettuce and cheese on the top right quarter.

4. Fold the tortilla in half from left to right. Then, fold the top part down. Enjoy your space burger!

GLOSSARY

celestial relating to the sky or outer space

collide to crash into something with force

dark matter a mysterious substance in space that we cannot see but that has effects on the universe

dollops small amounts of soft food

dust in cooking, to lightly coat a surface with flour to prevent sticking

garnish a decorative element added to a food or drink

gravity an invisible force that pulls objects toward one another

intervals spaces of time between events

irregular not having a clear or particular shape

pinwheel a toy with spiral arms that spin when air passes by

preheat to heat in advance to a set temperature

proof the resting period during which dough rises and becomes puffy

radiate to emit outward from a central point

whisk a kitchen utensil with wire loops used to beat a liquid

INDEX

allergy 5–6, 8, 12, 20
cheese 6–7, 12–13, 22
chocolate 8, 10–11, 14–17
clusters 4, 6, 8, 10–11, 20
dark matter 8
dust 6, 14
gas 6, 14, 18
gravity 6, 8
irregular galaxy 14, 17
punch 18–19
spiral galaxy 4, 12–13
Whitson, Peggy 22

READ MORE

Finan, Catherine C. *Stars and Galaxies (X-treme Facts: Space).* Minneapolis: Bearport Publishing, 2022.

Weider, Shoshana Z. *The Magic and Mystery of Space: Tour Across Our Astounding Universe.* New York: DK Children, 2025.

LEARN MORE ONLINE

1. Go to **FactSurfer.com** or scan the QR code below.
2. Enter "**Galaxy Recipes**" into the search box.
3. Click on the cover of this book to see a list of websites.

ABOUT THE AUTHOR

Jane Yates is an avid cook who worked in restaurants while attending art school. She has written more than 20 craft books for children.